Contents

Skits and Dramas

Songs and Poems

For Kids

CHRISTMAS

PROGRAMS, DRAMAS, and SKITS

Carpenter's Son Publishing

Christmas Programs, Dramas, and Skits: For Kids

©2015 by Paul Shepherd

Published by Carpenter's Son Publishing, Franklin, Tennessee.

Published in association with Larry Carpenter of Christian Book Services, LLC.
www.christianbookservices.com

Scripture is used from the New King James Version, © 1982 by Thomas Nelson, Inc. All rights reserved. Used by permission.

Scripture quotations marked (NIV) are taken from the Holy Bible, New International Version®, NIV®. Copyright © 1973, 1978, 1984, 2011 by Biblica, Inc.™ Used by permission of Zondervan. All rights reserved worldwide. www.zondervan.com.

Material used, with permission, from the following:
Diana C. Derringer, Shayna DuPré, Alice Sullivan, Kayleen Reusser, Charlotte Druitt Cole, David Teems, Nahum Tate, O. Henry, Rob Britt, Carlton W. Hughes, Jules Labadier, John Milton, William Canton, Elizabeth Cecilia Clephane, Charles Wesley, Isaac Watts, Dianne Garvis, Marjorie L. C. Pickthall, Eugene Field, John Wesley Work, Jr., and Edmund Sears

Edited by Alice Sullivan and Gail Fallen

Cover and Interior Layout Design by Suzanne Lawing

Printed in the United States of America

978-1-942587-14-9

Skits

and

Dramas

The Pirate Who Tried to Steal Christmas!

*Written through inspiration of the Holy Spirit
by Dianne Garvis © 2007*

NARRATOR: 'Twas the night before Christmas, when all through the house, not a creature was stirring, not even a mouse.

Music plays (some type of pirate music).

Choir enters—stomping in—singing pirate song.

NARRATOR: But this story starts upon the high sea; The pirates were restless due to the Captain's decree.

CAPTAIN BLYTHE: There'll be no more Christmas! No more holiday cheer! We'll pillage their toys. Their best Christmas was . . . LAST YEAR! Replace treasures with crossbones; leave skulls on their beds! No more visions of sugarplums will dance in their heads.

NARRATOR: The Captain summoned his first mate with a billowing shout! Snively came tottering, squeaking his words out.

SNIVELY: You called for me, Captain? What can I do?

CAPTAIN BLYTHE: Snively, it's time to gather me crew!

SNIVELY: Ye-e-es, Sir! Captain, you brilliant buccaneer, I'll gather the men and bring them right here.

NARRATOR: So off he did scurry, Captain Blythe he must please. When he got to the deck, the crew was scrubbing on their knees.

SNIVELY: Oh D-d-dear! Your cleaning is through. Captain Blythe said it's time to sail the Briny Blue.

NARRATOR: As they got to the bow, the sails began to quiver. The commands of this marauder would cause a rogue to shiver.

CAPTAIN BLYTHE: Cast off, you mangy dogs! Hoist anchor! Set sail! Another notch in me scabbard to hear sad children wail!

NARRATOR: Then from the top deck the crew heard him call,

CAPTAIN BLYTHE: Now cast away, cast away, cast away all!

Music track fades in slowly.

NARRATOR: Back on the mainland, families gathered in prayer. A celebration of Christmas, without even a care.

Choir sings medley of Christmas carols.

NARRATOR: At that precise moment, Captain Blythe did appear. It seems their genuine joy had brought him to tears. He was watching them worship, their Savior, the King, Perplexed for he thought they'd been greedy for things. This black-hearted scoundrel suddenly felt his heart ache, For he'd wasted his life; it was too much to take.

CAPTAIN BLYTHE: Arrrgh! Blast! I've been a babbling fool. I should walk the plank, for I've been so cruel.

NARRATOR: Then from across the room there came the smallest wee girl. Her face like an angel; her hair worn in curls.

LITTLE GIRL: What's wrong Mister Pirate? Please, sir. Don't cry.

NARRATOR: As she dried off his tears, she looked into his eye.

LITTLE GIRL: You see that little baby? Jesus is His name. To save us from death is the reason He came. He loves you, nice man, so please don't be sad. No one has ever been unforgivably bad.

NARRATOR: Captain spoke not a word. Sinking straight to his knees, overcome with repentance, he cried . . .

CAPTAIN BLYTHE: Father, forgive me. PLEASE!

NARRATOR: Then he sprang to his feet, feeling light as a feather.

He began to dance around exclaiming,

CAPTAIN BLYTHE: I feel SO MUCH BETTER!

NARRATOR: The town heard him proclaim as he sailed out of sigh . . .

CAPTAIN BLYTHE: Merry Christmas to ALL. And to ALL a Blessed Night!

Sound track begins—Final triumphant Christmas song.

Uprooted

by Diana C. Derringer © 2015

SUMMARY: *A Christmas tree relives the trauma and revelation of its Christmas experience.*

CHARACTER: *Christmas Tree*

SETTING: *a family room*

PROPS: *wrapped gifts, Nativity scene*

COSTUME: *green clothing, such as a stiff A-line dress; brown socks, or tights and shoes*

The Christmas Tree, surrounded by gifts and with a Nativity scene in front, speaks with agony.

CHRISTMAS TREE: How horrible! How absolutely horrible . . . the day the humans came, all bundled in their warm clothing, laughing and singing, with *(shudder)* those shovels over their shoulders. They walked through us, looking us over, discussing our shape and height like we weren't even there. And then they stopped right in front of me. *(shrink back)* Nodding their heads and saying I looked perfect, I began to relax . . . until the shoveling began. *(higher voice pitch)* Around and around and around they went with those shovels, digging deeper and deeper until they uncovered all my roots. *(shudder)* Then they pulled me completely out of the ground! I thought I was going to die!

They bundled my roots in a rough brown cloth and tied it around my trunk. I appreciated the warmth, but that didn't last long. They began dragging me away from the only home I'd ever known, laughing like they couldn't care less. Then they threw me on top of their car and tied me down on that hard metal top, and the agony only grew worse. As they drove away, the wind and snow beat on my branches. *(Sway from side to side.)* I thought they would never stop, but finally they pulled into a driveway. More humans came running out of the house to pull me off the car. Close behind them came two dogs and a cat determined to rip me to shreds.

Why? Why was this happening?

After the miserable cold, they took me inside the house to a room with a roaring fireplace. Whew! *(wipe brow)* Talk about a change! They spent a few more minutes admiring my beauty, *(adjust hair)* such as it was after that awful ride. Then they dumped my roots in a bucket—a bucket, for heaven's sake! No mountaintop, no sunrise or sunset, no other trees . . . There I stood: in a house in a cold metal bucket. *(pause)* I have to admit the dirt and water did provide some much-needed refreshment. I slurped that water faster than they could pour.

Then, yikes, what did they do next? They covered me in strands of little lights. Now, if that won't suck the moisture right out of your branches, I don't know what will. But they were just getting started. Next came box after box of glittery, sparkly, funny-looking objects, and they hung every single one on me. I wasn't a tree any longer. I was a billboard!

But slowly the mood changed. *(reverently, gesturing toward Nativity beneath)* Underneath my branches, they placed what looked like a little barn. Inside they arranged a few animals, a couple of humans, and then a baby in a feeding trough! Why would they place a baby in a feeding trough? *(pause)* Anyway, near the trough they placed more humans on their knees with their heads bowed.

As they talked about the meaning of all this, I listened carefully, and what an amazing story. They said that baby came to save the world. He gave up the splendor of heaven in order to sacrifice His life for others, and He teaches that everyone who follows Him must also die to self.

I wonder . . . I wonder if perhaps the giving of myself might also make a difference.

Lights out.

Michael and the Toy Truck

by Alice Sullivan © 2015

SUMMARY: *Children in Mrs. Fay's classroom learn that Christmas is about the birth of a Savior, not about pretty decorations.*

PREMISE: *All the children in the Mother's Day Out program are helping their teacher decorate the Christmas tree—but one. Michael, a soft-spoken boy, keeps taking decorations off the tree, putting them in the bed of his toy dump truck, and driving to the other side of the room. When the teacher becomes frustrated that Michael keeps taking the decorations away, she asks him what he plans to do with the ornaments. His answer—to make a soft bed for baby Jesus—melts her heart, and another child, Ellie, brings her doll over to Michael. He wraps it in a white paper towel and puts it in the back of the truck on top of the ornaments.*

CHARACTERS:

Mrs. Fay, teacher
Children:
Ellie: child with doll
Grayson
Lucy
Zack
Michael: child with the toy truck

DIRECTOR'S NOTE: *Children may be called by their real names, if preferred.*

SETTING: *children's classroom*

PROPS: *Christmas tree, ornaments, box or bucket for ornaments, large toy dump truck (or similar toy with a bed), doll, white paper towels*

All the children (but Michael) are gathered around the tree helping Mrs. Fay hang the ornaments. Michael is playing with his toy truck a few feet away.

Scene 1

MRS. FAY: Ellie, that's a beautiful ornament! Yes, place it right next to the silver bells.

ELLIE: Like this?

MRS. FAY: Perfect! Zack, which one have you picked out?

ZACK: I have a snowman! I'm going to put him high on a limb so he can see everything.

MRS. FAY: Wonderful!

Children continue to select and hang ornaments. Michael scoots in with his toy truck, takes a few ornaments off the tree and places them in the back of his truck, and scoots away again to the side of the room. He continues playing alone. Mrs. Fay notices, but doesn't say anything.

MRS. FAY: Grayson, what's your favorite ornament?

GRAYSON: I like this reindeer! He has a red nose like a clown.

MRS. FAY: That's Rudolph the Red-Nosed Reindeer!

GRAYSON: He looks like my dog, Ollie!

Grayson plays with his ornament a bit and then places it on the tree.

MRS. FAY: That's sweet. Lucy—

Michael scoots over and takes a few more ornaments off the tree, places them in the bed of his toy truck, and scoots away. Mrs. Fay is flustered.

MRS. FAY: Um . . . Lucy, which ornament is your favorite?

LUCY: I like the snowflakes best. Mamma says every one is different, and they're fun to catch on your tongue!

MRS. FAY: That's exactly right! No two snowflakes are alike. Just like people.

Michael comes by a third time to take ornaments, and Mrs. Fay finally says something.

MRS. FAY: Michael, what are you doing? Why are you taking the ornaments off the tree? Don't you want to help decorate for Christmas?

MICHAEL: I am.

MRS. FAY: You are what?

MICHAEL: I am decorating.

MRS. FAY: What are you decorating?

MICHAEL: I'm decorating a bed for baby Jesus.

All children stop and look over at the bed of the truck, filled with ornaments.

ZACK: You can't put a baby in there. He'd fall out!

MICHAEL: No he won't. See? I put all the soft ornaments on the bottom and the bigger ones on the side.

MRS. FAY: Michael, that's so sweet, but why does baby Jesus need a bed?

All children are gathered around the toy truck now. Some are kneeling.

MICHAEL: He's a special baby, the Son of God, and He brings good news to us all.

All characters pause, and lights go out. Offstage, someone reads Luke 2:1–14 aloud. Lights come back on after the reading.

GRAYSON: So, where's the baby?

ELLIE: I have a doll!

Ellie runs to her cubby (or table) and grabs her doll. She places it in the back of the truck, on top of the ornaments.

ZACK: *(makes a face)* This doesn't look right.

MICHAEL: I know what we need!

Michael runs to the side of the room, grabs a roll of paper towels, and returns. Then he wraps the doll in paper towels and places it on the ornaments.

LUCY: That looks cozy!

MRS. FAY: Children, this is just beautiful. Why don't we all sing a Christmas song? What about "Silent Night"?

ALL CHILDREN: Yeah!

Children begin to sing and lights fade out.

Santa Falls Short

by Diana C. Derringer © 2015

SUMMARY: *A child contemplates the shortcomings of Santa when compared to Jesus.*

CHARACTER: *Child*

SETTING: *a child's bedroom*

PROPS: *a ragged stuffed animal*

COSTUME: *contemporary child's clothing*

The Child sits on the floor, holding and talking to a stuffed animal.

CHILD: Just think, Rags, only five more days till Christmas! Are you excited? *(Shake animal's head up and down.)* Me too! *(forefinger under chin)* I wonder what Santa will bring this year. Maybe he'll have a new friend for you. Would you like that? *(Shake animal's head up and down.)* What fun we could have! *(Hug animal tightly.)* But nobody will ever take your place. Don't you worry about that.

(Start singing "Santa Claus is Coming to Town," then stop suddenly.) You know what, Rags? I've been thinking a lot lately, and some things about Santa sorta' bother me. I mean, why does he only show up once a year? If he loves

us and wants to give us good stuff, why wait till Christmas? We might need him other times too. Mommy says Jesus stays with us all the time and never leaves us. I think I like that plan better.

And you know what else? Santa only brings us presents if we're good, and a few times I've not been so sure if I would get anything! Do you know how hard it is for little kids to be good all the time? *(Pause, holding animal out.)* Trust me, it's not easy! But Mommy says Jesus loves us just the way we are, no matter what! That's a relief. Of course, Mommy also says Jesus wants us to be good and will help us be good if we let Him in our lives. I don't know all about that yet, but Mommy says I will when the time is right.

And why does Santa come sneaking down chimneys in the middle of the night when everybody's sleeping? Looks like he would just walk right up to the door in broad daylight and say, *(Raise one arm of stuffed animal.)* "Hi, I'm Santa, and here's your present." Wouldn't that be great? Of course, I can't see Jesus either, but I can talk to Him any time I want to. If I get scared of storms, or I'm playing, or I'm getting ready to eat bananas and peanut butter, or I fall off the swing, or I'm all dressed for bed, I can talk to Jesus and He listens. If I need to watch what I'm doing, I don't even have to close my eyes and bow my head. He listens anyway. Want me to show you? *(Look up, smiling and lifting animal.)* "Hi, Jesus, this is my best friend, Rags." *(Lower head and look at Rags.)* See, wasn't that easy?

Rags, have you noticed how Santa talks? About all he says is, *(lower voice)* "Ho, ho, ho, have you been a good little boy or girl?" That's not much, is it? But there's a whole book just filled with stuff Jesus said. Things like be kind to other people, and He loves us, and He'll help us when we mess up . . . so many good things, I can't even remember them all. How about that?

I guess maybe Santa tries the best he can, but seems to me he could learn some great lessons from Jesus. Probably we all could, huh?

Skip off stage, holding Rags.

Away in a Manger

by Kayleen Reusser © 2015

SUMMARY: *An examination of Jesus' manger shows us an example of God's love.*

CHARACTERS:
Joseph and Mary
Narrator, offstage
Singer, offstage

COSTUMES: *Biblical time attire for Mary, Joseph*

SETTING: *Barn stall resembling a cave. A feeding trough is part of the cave.*

PROPS: *Baby doll wrapped in cloths, straw, trash can*

Soft light on Joseph and Mary sitting in cave setting onstage. Mary holds baby.

SINGER: Away in a manger,
no crib for His bed,
the little Lord Jesus
laid down His sweet head.
The stars in the sky
looked down where He lay,
the little Lord Jesus,
asleep on the hay.

NARRATOR: "And she gave birth to her firstborn, a son. She wrapped him in cloths and placed him in a manger" *(Luke 2:7, aloud).*

When we think of the Nativity scene, we picture Mary, Joseph, shepherds, and a sheep or two surrounding baby Jesus. Baby Jesus sleeps peacefully in a manger filled with fresh, clean-smelling straw. The scene looks calm and idyllic.

In reality, the scene was probably quite unlike that when Jesus was born. If anyone has been in a barn with animals, they know it is not quiet and certainly not sweet-smelling. Jesus was born in a setting designed for large animals, not people. *(Lights up on cave setting around the couple. Sounds of animals mooing and baaing are heard offstage. Straw is scattered around.)*

NARRATOR: Some other details may be different than we have been led to believe. Some Bible scholars believe the innkeeper may have offered Mary and Joseph refuge in one of the caves surrounding Bethlehem. It was common for people in that region to use caves to shelter their animals. Out of desperation, they accepted, and Mary gave birth to God's Son inside. The Bible tells us Mary laid Jesus in a manger, or feeding trough, for animals. The manger may not have been wooden as we might think, but carved into the wall of a cave. Most caves were formed by erosion of the area's soft limestone, and herdsmen carved niches for feeding troughs. Joseph would have covered it with straw or clean grass, and this primitive spot was possibly where Mary placed baby Jesus. *(Mary places doll in manger.)*

SINGER: The cattle are lowing,
the poor Baby wakes.

But little Lord Jesus,
no crying He makes.
I love Thee, Lord Jesus,
look down from the sky.
And stay by my cradle
till morning is nigh.

NARRATOR: It is strange the Bible even mentions a manger. A carved-out niche in a cave wall would not have been thought of with respect in those days and certainly as no place to shelter a newborn baby. Today it would be as if Jesus were laid in a trash can. *(Spotlight on trash can.)* The thought makes us shudder.

Yet God chose a manger for the birthplace of His Son.

Why would God allow his newborn Son to be placed in a despised, unimportant place? Maybe it was because God wanted us to know He specializes in taking the ordinary, dirty, and forgotten and making them extraordinary. *(Spotlight back on Joseph, Mary watching baby in manger.)* Only God could transform a manger into an object of love, security, peace, and hope.

He is willing to do the same with our lives. When we place our dirty mangers into His hands—anger, gossipy spirit, thoughts of envy—He transforms them by the Holy Spirit into something holy and pleasing to God.

If you have a dirty manger in your life, this Christmas season ask God to transform it into something beautiful for His glory. That could be the best present you ever receive.

SINGER: Be near me, Lord Jesus,
I ask Thee to stay,

Close by me forever,
and love me, I pray!
Bless all the dear children
in Thy tender care
And take us to heaven,
to Live with Thee there.*

Lights out.

* "Away in a Manger," words, anon.; music, James R. Murray, in *Dainty Songs for Little Lads and Lasses* (Cincinnati, OH: The John Church Co., 1887), n.p.

Birthday Presents

by Diana C. Derringer © 2015

SUMMARY: *Children learn that they give to Jesus when they give to people in need.*

CHARACTERS:
Ms. Linda, teacher
Children:
Kelsey
Corey
Lexi
Grace
Seth
Levi

DIRECTOR'S NOTE: *Children may be called by their real names, if preferred.*

SETTING: *children's classroom*

PROPS: *quilt, snack food, a large banner that reads "One Week Later," Bible, baby blanket, toy, food, baby clothes, board books, piggy bank*

COSTUMES: *contemporary winter clothing*

Ms. Linda and the children sit on the quilt in a circle. Lexi munches on snack food throughout the scene.

Scene 1

MS. LINDA: Who knows what holiday we're celebrating?

All the children's hands fly in the air, and they start calling, "Christmas," with a few also saying, "Jesus' birthday."

MS. LINDA: That's right. We're celebrating Christmas, a day to remember Jesus' birth. We don't really know what day Jesus was born, but December twenty-fifth is the day we celebrate. I'm wondering, how does your family celebrate Christmas?

Children's hands go up.

MS. LINDA: Yes, Kelsey?

KELSEY: We put up a Christmas tree.

MS. LINDA: Great one. What about the rest of you? How many have a Christmas tree?

All raise their hands.

MS. LINDA: What else do you do for Jesus' birthday? Corey, what does your family do?

COREY: We bake a cake and sing "Happy Birthday" to Jesus.

MS. LINDA: Oh, I like that idea. Does anyone else do that?

Lexi and Grace raise their hands.

MS. LINDA: Wonderful! What else? Seth, what about your family?

SETH: We go to my grandma's house on Christmas Eve.

MS. LINDA: I'd say a lot of you visit relatives during Christmas, don't you?

Heads nod.

MS. LINDA: Levi, we haven't heard from you yet. What does your family do?

LEVI: We drive all over the place and look at all the Christmas lights. Have you seen the lights at the park? Wow! They're amazing! You've got to go see them. *(The longer he talks, the louder and faster he goes.)* They have Santa and Rudolph and the wise men and the shepherds and angels and baby Jesus in a manger and stars and elves and gingerbread people and—

MS. LINDA: *(laughing)* I think we get the picture, Levi. How many of you have seen the decorations at the park?

All hands go up.

MS. LINDA: Well, look at that, Levi. A lot of your friends enjoy those amazing lights too.

Levi nods his head enthusiastically.

MS. LINDA: What about other Christmas traditions?

KELSEY: We set out a Nativ . . . a Nativ . . . oh, you know, baby Jesus with Mary and Joseph and the sheep and everybody.

MS. LINDA: A Nativity scene.

KELSEY: That's it, a Nativity scene. Actually, we have several all over the house, and you know what?

MS. LINDA: What?

KELSEY: Instead of putting the wise men next to baby Jesus, we put them on the other side of the room. You know why?

MS. LINDA: *(smiling)* Why?

KELSEY: Because my daddy said the wise men had a long, long trip. He said Jesus was probably about two years old and living in a house before they ever found Him.

SETH: Wow, that is a long trip!

KELSEY: And they had to make it on camels too.

MS. LINDA: You're daddy's right, Kelsey. Although most people put their wise men next to baby Jesus, He probably was a little boy before they arrived. I may have to start your family's tradition with my Nativity scene. I like that idea. *(pause)* If I remember correctly, everyone said you have a Christmas tree, right? What do you put under your tree?

ALL CHILDREN: Presents!

MS. LINDA: And who gets those presents?

ALL CHILDREN: We do!

MS. LINDA: Hmm. I'm a little confused. Whose birthday is it?

ALL CHILDREN: *(a little quieter)* Jesus.

MS. LINDA: And who gets the presents?

ALL CHILDREN: *(still quieter)* We do.

COREY: Ms. Linda, that's not right. If it's Jesus' birthday, why don't we buy gifts for Him?

MS. LINDA: Good question, Corey. *(looking around at the group)* Everyone, if you could have taken a gift to Jesus when He was born, what would you have taken? Kelsey, you start.

KELSEY: A warm blanket.

MS. LINDA: Great idea, Kelsey. Babies need to stay warm.

COREY: A toy.

MS. LINDA: Yes, all babies should have a toy, shouldn't they, Corey?

LEXI: Something to eat.

MS. LINDA: *(smiling)* Of course, Lexi. We all need to eat.

GRACE: Some clothes.

MS. LINDA: Good thinking, Grace. Jesus' mother wrapped Him in strips of cloth when He was first born, but we couldn't leave Him in those forever, could we?

SETH: Books, so Mary and Joseph could read to Him.

MS. LINDA: Don't you just love to read, Seth? And you know what? One of the best ways we learn to read is if our parents read to us when we're little.

LEXI: I would give Jesus' family some money, so they could find a better place to stay.

MS. LINDA: How thoughtful, Lexi. A stable provided Mary, Joseph, and baby Jesus shelter, but newborn babies definitely need a cleaner, safer place to live. *(Pause, looking around at everyone.)* I love all your gift ideas. Why don't you bring what you mentioned with you next week, and we'll give those gifts to Jesus?

GRACE: But Ms. Linda, how can we give them to Jesus? He

lives in heaven.

MS. LINDA: Just trust me on this, okay, Grace? Bring your gifts next week, and we'll celebrate Jesus' birthday by giving all of them to Him.

Lights out.

Scene 2

Two children carry the banner reading "One Week Later" across the stage. Everyone returns to previous positions with their gifts.

MS. LINDA: Wonderful! Everyone remembered your gifts for Jesus. Before we give them to Him, I need a volunteer to read a verse from the Bible.

SETH: I will, Ms. Linda.

MS. LINDA: Thank you, Seth. *(Hand him an open Bible.)* Here you go. Read Matthew 25:40.

SETH: "The King will reply, 'Truly I tell you, whatever you did for one of the least of these brothers and sisters of mine, you did for me.'"

MS. LINDA: Who do you suppose "the King" is here?

SETH: Jesus?

MS. LINDA: You're exactly right, Seth. So what's Jesus telling us?

LEXI: *(uncertainly)* When we do something to help somebody in need, we're doing that for Jesus?

MS. LINDA: Absolutely, Lexi! So what do we need to do with the gifts we brought for Jesus?

LEXI: *(excited)* Give them to someone who needs them!

MS. LINDA: Right again! And when we do that, we are giving them to Jesus. Now, let's put our heads together and decide who will get these gifts for Jesus.

Everyone moves closer together and starts talking quietly.

Lights out.

Christmas Wrapping Paper Caper

by Alice Sullivan © 2015

PREMISE: *While the mom is trying to wrap presents in her room, she notices the wrapping paper keeps disappearing. She's becoming frustrated. However, when she comes out to investigate, she sees the kids are wrapping themselves as gifts, as well as the family dog. Mom takes a break to tell her kids and the family dog, Pips, what special gifts they are to her.*

CHARACTERS:

Mom: wrapping Christmas presents in her room
Dillon: son who grabs the extra tape dispenser and bows
Bree: daughter who is sneaking the rolls of wrapping paper out of Mom's room
Pips: family dog

DIRECTOR'S NOTE: *Children may be called by their real names, if preferred.*

SETTING: *house with two rooms: one as a bedroom or kitchen, and the other a living room with Christmas decorations such as a tree. It is a few days before Christmas.*

PROPS: *dog (or child dressed as dog), tape dispensers, kid-friendly scissors (two pair), several tubes of wrapping paper, bows, table for wrapping gifts, boxes/gifts to wrap. If using a real dog, just let him roam free most of the skit until he needs to have a bow put on his/her head or around the neck. If a* child dressed as a dog, he/she can follow the kids each time they go to Mom's room.

Scene 1

Mom is putting boxes of Christmas gifts on a table to prepare them to be wrapped. As she's deciding which gifts to wrap first and looking through her many rolls of wrapping paper, the kids are whispering to each other close by, planning their sneaky surprise.

MOM: *(humming Christmas carols to herself)* Look at all these great presents! I hope Dillon and Bree like what we got them. I can't wait to see what Santa brings everyone too! I know they've been good this year. *(She takes the biggest box first, selects some wrapping paper, and starts to cut it to size.)*

DILLON: *(to Bree)* Do you see that big box? I wonder what's in it. Maybe it's a puppy!

BREE: *(hushes Dillon)* Shhhh! Don't let Mom hear you. I bet it isn't a puppy. The box isn't jumping around. Maybe it is a new computer!

DILLON: No, no. Hey! Do you see that bag of bows on the table? I bet if we're quiet, you can grab the paper, I can grab the bag, and we can start wrapping Mom's gifts!

BREE: Okay! I'll go first! *(Bree crawls quietly to the table, reaches up, grabs a roll of wrapping paper, and crawls back to the other room.)*

DILLON: Great! Now we need some pretty bows! I'll get them. *(Dillon crawls to the table, grabs some bows, and quietly* *crawls back to the other room. Mom looks up, looks at the table, and seems confused.)*

MOM: Hmm. I thought I had more paper than this. *(Then she goes back to wrapping.)*

BREE: We have paper and bows, but how are we going to cut the paper?

DILLON: We need scissors! I think I saw an extra pair on the table. I'll be right back. *(Dillon belly crawls on the floor to the table like he's a spy, pops his hand up, feels around for the scissors, and comes back.)*

BREE: Yay! Now we have scissors! Wait . . . we don't have any tape! Can we use gum?

DILLON: No, I don't have enough gum. Plus, Pips would just eat it.

BREE: Okay, I'll go get the tape. *(She crawls to the table and takes the extra tape. She crawls back without being caught. Bree and Dillon disappear offstage with the supplies.)*

Scene 2

Mom is now on her second or third gift, and she notices she's running out of tape. She calls to the kids, but they don't answer. She's starting to get suspicious that they're up to something.

MOM: Bree? Dillon? Have you seen my tape? I had some extra tape right here *(She turns all the way around in a circle.)* . . . at least I thought I did. *(She looks under the table too.)* Guess I need to get some more tape out of the closet!

She walks offstage, and as she does, Dillon runs into the room and snatches another roll of paper. He is wearing a cape made of wrapping paper and a bow on his head, like a king. He leaves the room just as Mom walks back in.

DILLON: *(to Bree)* Whew! Got it! That was close!

MOM: *(looks down at the table)* Now how is that possible? I had another roll of paper right here! Maybe I'm just imagining things. I hope the kids aren't playing a trick on me. *(She goes back to wrapping gifts.)*

Scene 3

Mom is almost finished wrapping gifts but now needs more wrapping paper and goes offstage to grab another roll. As she does, Bree hops in, her legs wrapped together in paper . . . like a potato sack race. She grabs another roll and hops off just as Mom comes back to the room.

MOM: What in the world?! How is the paper disappearing? Kids! Are you taking my paper and tape and scissors? That's not a very nice thing to do. *(She walks into the other room to see the kids and the dog totally wrapped up in paper.)*

BREE AND DILLON (AND PIPS): Surprise!

MOM: What is this?

BREE: We wanted to wrap Christmas presents for you!

DILLON: Yeah! And we are all we had!

BREE: Pips likes his bow! *(Pips can wear a bow on his head or a bow around his neck.)*

MOM: *(Hugging both kids close.)* You kids are the best gift a mom could have . . . and you did a very nice job of wrapping yourselves! *(looks at Pips)* You too, Pips! Next year you can wrap all the gifts!

Everyone walks off stage. Lights out.

What's the Big Deal about a Baby?

by Diana C. Derringer © 2015

SUMMARY: *A stranger unfamiliar with Christmas arrives in an area caught up in the annual celebration and calls home after observing the festivities for several days.*

CHARACTER: *The Stranger, an older child, origin unknown*

SETTING: *a small park*

PROPS: *several decorated Christmas trees, a bench in center front, a cell phone*

COSTUME: *any strange combination of clothing, shoes, backpack, and hat*

A cell phone rings. The Stranger runs to the park bench, digs through the backpack, finds the phone, and answers with great enthusiasm and animation.

THE STRANGER: Hey, Mom! How are you? Me, I'm great—a little tired, but, wow, what fun! Almost every night we go somewhere different and eat until we're ready to pop! Funny-shaped cookies, all kinds of candy, dips and chips—you name it, they have it. (*Wave free arm to emphasize descriptions.*) Sometimes families have these huge dinners with enough food to last a week!

Children write letters and visit a really fat old man with

white hair and a beard. He dresses mostly in red. They give him long lists of everything they want and then wait for his visit to all of them in one night! *(Prop chin with free hand and frown.)* I think I have this figured out though. I've noticed several men dressed exactly alike, so I believe they work together. However, they call all of them by the same name, *(scratch head)* and that's a bit confusing.

(Jump up with greater animation, pantomiming actions discussed.) Actually, a lot of people dress in red or green. They also decorate their houses with bright colors and thousands of tiny lights. They put trees *(Run toward one of the decorated trees and pretend to decorate.)* inside their houses and hang lights and cute little decorations on them. *(The excitement builds.)* And you can't believe how much they buy—clothes, food, toys, and all sorts of unusual gadgets with no real value or purpose. *(movement stops, hand under chin, brow wrinkled)* The really weird thing? A lot of people don't seem to enjoy shopping but do it anyway. Then they wrap this stuff in shiny paper and ribbons and give it to people who give them useless stuff in return. *(Throw hand up in confusion.)*

(Take three or four steps and pause.) A few people sing a lot, *(Wave hand, as though directing music.)* sometimes in big groups in buildings called churches, other times in smaller groups going from house to house in the cold. Although they do this at night, no one seems frightened by them. In fact, some families invite the singers inside for . . . what else . . . another round of snacks.

Kids my age get more and more hyper. Their parents get more and more stressed.

When I asked someone why they do all this, he said it's because a baby named Jesus was born. *(Pause, sit on bench, cross legs, elbow on knees, chin in hand.)* I don't get it. *(Stand suddenly, throwing free hand upward.)* What's the big deal about a baby anyway? And what does a baby have to do with all these strange customs?

Oops, our chaperone says we have to go. Time for another party and more food!

Return phone to backpack and exit quickly.

Songs and Poems

A Child's Song of Christmas*

by Marjorie L. C. Pickthall (1883–1922)

My counterpane is soft as silk,
My blankets white as creamy milk.
The hay was soft to Him, I know,
Our little Lord of long ago.

Above the roofs the pigeons fly
In silver wheels across the sky.
The stable-doves they cooed to them,
Mary and Christ in Bethlehem.

Bright shines the sun across the drifts,
And bright upon my Christmas gifts.
They brought Him incense, myrrh, and gold,
Our little Lord who lived of old.

Oh, soft and clear our mother sings
Of Christmas joys and Christmas things.
God's holy angels sang to them,
Mary and Christ in Bethlehem.

Our hearts they hold all Christmas dear,
And earth seems sweet and heaven seems near,
Oh, heaven was in His sight, I know,
That little Child of long ago.

---

* Marjorie L. C. Pickthall, "The Drift of Pinions," *The University Magazine* (1913), 54.

The First Noel

Traditional English Carol, c. Sixteenth Century

The First Noel, the Angels did say
Was to certain poor shepherds in fields as they lay:
In fields where they lay keeping their sheep
On a cold winter's night that was so deep.
Noel, Noel, Noel, Noel,
Born is the King of Israel!

They looked up and saw a star
Shining in the East beyond them far:
And to the earth it gave great light
And so it continued both day and night.
Noel, Noel, Noel, Noel,
Born is the King of Israel!

And by the light of that same star
Three Wise men came from country far;
To seek for a King was their intent
And to follow the star wherever it went.
Noel, Noel, Noel, Noel,
Born is the King of Israel!

This star drew nigh to the northwest;
O'er Bethlehem it took its rest,
And there it did both stop and stay,
Right o'er the place where Jesus lay.
Noel, Noel, Noel, Noel
Born is the King of Israel!

Then entered in those Wise men three,
Full reverently upon their knee,
And offered there in His presence
Their gold and myrrh and frankincense.
Noel, Noel, Noel, Noel,
Born is the King of Israel!

Then let us all with one accord
Sing praises to our heavenly Lord,
That hath made Heaven and earth of naught,
And with his blood mankind has bought.
Noel, Noel, Noel, Noel,
Born is the King of Israel!

Significant Though Small

by Diana C. Derringer © 2010

One little town,
yet a single event
changed the world and its history
through the Son who was sent.

One ray of light
in a star-studded sky
gave direction to those searching
for God's Promise brought nigh.

One unknown girl
without status or fame
became mother of Messiah
as the angel proclaimed.

One tiny baby
with no bed of His own
was the Good News incarnate.
God's mercy was shown.

Any life, deemed by others
as meaningless and small,
gains significance and purpose
by following His call.

To Love Is Christ*

by David Teems

"For behold, henceforth all generations will call me blessed. For He who is mighty has done great things for me, and holy is His name" (Luke 1:46–49, NKJV).

She was the first to know, the first to hear from angels' lips the gospel of His coming. The first to hold Him. The first to feel His hunger. The first to know the gentle rhythms of His heart. When love sought a door, a passage of entry, a mother to child itself into this world, she offered up her will, her consent, her body. And Christianity had its first stirrings, cradled in the surrender and in the womb of a maiden.

**In Jesus, the son of Mary and
the Christ within her, Amen.**

May you enjoy all the blessings that have assigned to you, as well as some you never would have expected, for heaven is full of surprises when it mingles with things of Earth and faithfulness.

---

* David Teems, *To Love Is Christ* (Nashville, TN: Thomas Nelson, 2009), n.p.

Why Do the Bells of Christmas Ring?*

by Eugene Field

Why do the bells of Christmas ring?
Why do little children sing?
Once a lovely shining star,
Seen by shepherds from afar,
Gently moved until its light
Made a manger's cradle bright.
There a darling baby lay,
Pillowed soft upon the hay;
And its mother sung and smiled:
This is Christ, the holy Child!
Therefore bells for Christmas ring,
Therefore little children sing.

---

* Eugene Field, "Why Do the Bells of Christmas Ring?" in *Christmas Tales and Christmas Verse,* illus. Florence Storer (New York, NY: Charles Scribner's Sons, 1912), n.p.

Go Tell It on the Mountain!

African-American Spiritual
Compiled by John Wesley Work Jr., c. 1865

While shepherds kept their watching
Over silent flocks by night,
Behold throughout the heavens,
There shone a holy light:
Go, Tell It On The Mountain,
Over the hills and everywhere;
Go, Tell It On The Mountain
That Jesus Christ is born.

The shepherds feared and trembled
When lo! above the earth
Rang out the angel chorus
That hailed our Saviour's birth:
Go, Tell It On The Mountain,
Over the hills and everywhere;
Go, Tell It On The Mountain
That Jesus Christ is born.

Down in a lowly manger
Our humble Christ was born
And God send us salvation,
That blessed Christmas morn:
Go, Tell It On The Mountain,
Over the hills and everywhere;
Go, Tell It On The Mountain
That Jesus Christ is born.

When I am a seeker,
I seek both night and day;
I seek the Lord to help me,
And He shows me the way:
Go, Tell It On The Mountain,
Over the hills and everywhere;
Go, Tell It On The Mountain
That Jesus Christ is born.

He made me a watchman
Upon the city wall,
And if I am a Christian,
I am the least of all.
Go, Tell It On The Mountain,
Over the hills and everywhere;
Go, Tell It On The Mountain
That Jesus Christ is born.

It Came Upon the Midnight Clear

by Edmund Sears, c. 1849

It came upon the midnight clear,
That glorious song of old,
From angels bending near the earth,
To touch their harps of gold:

"Peace on the earth, good will to men,
From heaven's all-gracious King."
The world in solemn stillness lay,
To hear the angels sing.

Still through the cloven skies they come,
With peaceful wings unfurled,
And still their heavenly music floats
Over all the weary world;

Above its sad and lowly plains,
They bend on hovering wing,
And ever over its babel-sounds
The blessed angels sing.

Yet with the woes of sin and strife
The world has suffered long;
Beneath the heavenly strain have rolled
Two thousand years of wrong;

And man, at war with man, hears not
The tidings which they bring;
O hush the noise, ye men of strife,
And hear the angels sing.

O ye, beneath life's crushing load,
Whose forms are bending low,
Who toil along the climbing way
With painful steps and slow.

Look now, for glad and golden hours
Come swiftly on the wing.
O rest beside the weary road,
And hear the angels sing!

For lo, the days are hastening on,
By prophets seen of old,
When with the ever-circling years
Shall come the time foretold

When peace shall over all the earth
Its ancient splendors fling,
And the whole world give back the song
Which now the angels sing.

The Gift of the Magi*

by O. Henry

One dollar and eighty-seven cents. That was all. And sixty cents of it was in pennies. Pennies saved one and two at a time by bulldozing the grocer and the vegetable man and the butcher until one's cheeks burned with the silent imputation of parsimony that such close dealing implied. Three times Della counted it. One dollar and eighty-seven cents. And the next day would be Christmas.

There was clearly nothing to do but flop down on the shabby little couch and howl. So Della did it. Which instigates the moral reflection that life is made up of sobs, sniffles, and smiles, with sniffles predominating.

While the mistress of the home is gradually subsiding from the first stage to the second, take a look at the home. A furnished flat at $8 per week. It did not exactly beggar description, but it certainly had that word on the lookout for the mendicancy squad.

In the vestibule below was a letter-box into which no letter would go, and an electric button from which no mortal finger could coax a ring. Also appertaining thereunto was a card bearing the name "Mr. James Dillingham Young."

The "Dillingham" had been flung to the breeze during a former period of prosperity when its possessor was being paid $30 per week. Now, when the income was shrunk to $20, the letters of "Dillingham" looked blurred, as though they were thinking seriously of contracting to a modest and unassuming D. But whenever Mr. James Dillingham Young came home and reached his flat above he was called "Jim" and greatly hugged by Mrs. James Dillingham Young, already introduced to you as Della. Which is all very good.

Della finished her cry and attended to her cheeks with the powder rag. She stood by the window and looked out dully at a gray cat walking a gray fence in a gray backyard. Tomorrow would be Christmas Day, and she had only $1.87 with which to buy Jim a present. She had been saving every penny she could for months, with this result. Twenty dollars a week doesn't go far. Expenses had been greater than she had calculated. They always are. Only $1.87 to buy a present for Jim. Her Jim. Many a happy hour she had spent planning for something nice for him. Something fine and rare and sterling—something just a little bit near to being worthy of the honor of being owned by Jim.

There was a pier-glass between the windows of the room. Perhaps you have seen a pier-glass in an $8 flat. A very thin and very agile person may, by observing his reflection in a rapid sequence of longitudinal strips, obtain a fairly accurate conception of his looks. Della, being slender, had mastered the art.

Suddenly she whirled from the window and stood before the glass. Her eyes were shining brilliantly, but her face had lost its color within twenty seconds. Rapidly she pulled down her hair and let it fall to its full length.

Now, there were two possessions of the James Dillingham Youngs in which they both took a mighty pride. One was Jim's gold watch that had been his father's and his grandfather's. The other was Della's hair. Had the Queen of Sheba lived in the flat across the airshaft, Della would have let her hair hang out the window some day to dry just to depreciate Her Majesty's jewels and gifts. Had King Solomon been the janitor, with all his treasures piled up in the basement, Jim would have pulled out his watch every time he passed, just to see him pluck at his beard from envy.

So now Della's beautiful hair fell about her rippling and shining like a cascade of brown waters. It reached below her knee and made itself almost a garment for her. And then she did it up again nervously and quickly. Once she faltered for a minute and stood still while a tear or two splashed on the worn red carpet.

On went her old brown jacket; on went her old brown hat. With a whirl of skirts and with the brilliant sparkle still in her eyes, she fluttered out the door and down the stairs to the street.

Where she stopped the sign read: "Mme. Sofronie. Hair Goods of All Kinds." One flight up Della ran, and collected herself, panting. Madame, large, too white, chilly, hardly looked the "Sofronie."

"Will you buy my hair?" asked Della.

"I buy hair," said Madame. "Take yer hat off and let's have a sight at the looks of it." Down rippled the brown cascade. "Twenty dollars," said Madame, lifting the mass with a practised hand.

"Give it to me quick," said Della.

Oh, and the next two hours tripped by on rosy wings. Forget the hashed metaphor. She was ransacking the stores for Jim's present.

She found it at last. It surely had been made for Jim and no one else. There was no other like it in any of the stores, and she had turned all of them inside out. It was a platinum fob chain simple and chaste in design, properly proclaiming its value by substance alone and not by meretricious ornamentation—as all good things should do. It was even worthy of The Watch. As soon as she saw it she knew that it must be Jim's. It was like him. Quietness and value—the description applied to both. Twenty-one dollars they took from her for it, and she hurried home with the 87 cents. With that chain on his watch Jim might be properly anxious about the time in any company. Grand as the watch was, he sometimes looked at it on the sly on account of the old leather strap that he used in place of a chain.

When Della reached home her intoxication gave way a little to prudence and reason. She got out her curling irons and lighted the gas and went to work repairing the ravages made by generosity added to love. Which is always a tremendous task, dear friends—a mammoth task.

Within forty minutes her head was covered with tiny, close-lying curls that made her look wonderfully like a truant schoolboy. She looked at her reflection in the mirror long, carefully, and critically.

"If Jim doesn't kill me," she said to herself, "before he takes a second look at me, he'll say I look like a Coney Island chorus girl. But what could I do—oh! what could I do with a dollar and eighty-seven cents?"

At 7 o'clock the coffee was made and the frying-pan was on the back of the stove hot and ready to cook the chops.

Jim was never late. Della doubled the fob chain in her hand and sat on the corner of the table near the door that he always entered. Then she heard his step on the stair away down on the first flight, and she turned white for just a moment. She had a habit of saying little silent prayers about the simplest everyday things, and now she whispered: "Please God, make him think I am still pretty."

The door opened and Jim stepped in and closed it. He looked thin and very serious. Poor fellow, he was only twenty-two—and to be burdened with a family! He needed a new overcoat and he was without gloves.

Jim stopped inside the door, as immovable as a setter at the scent of quail. His eyes were fixed upon Della, and there was an expression in them that she could not read, and it terrified her. It was not anger, nor surprise, nor disapproval, nor horror, nor any of the sentiments that she had been prepared for. He simply stared at her fixedly with that peculiar expression on his face.

Della wriggled off the table and went for him.

"Jim, darling," she cried, "don't look at me that way. I had my hair cut off and sold it because I couldn't have lived through Christmas without giving you a present. It'll grow out again—you won't mind, will you? I just had to do it. My hair grows awfully fast. Say 'Merry Christmas!' Jim, and let's be happy. You don't know what a nice—what a beautiful, nice gift I've got for you."

"You've cut off your hair?" asked Jim, laboriously, as if he had not arrived at that patent fact yet even after the hardest mental labor.

"Cut it off and sold it," said Della. "Don't you like me just as well, anyhow? I'm me without my hair, ain't I?"

Jim looked about the room curiously.

"You say your hair is gone?" he said, with an air almost of idiocy.

"You needn't look for it," said Della. "It's sold, I tell you—sold and gone, too. It's Christmas Eve, boy. Be good to me, for it went for you. Maybe the hairs of my head were numbered," she went on with a sudden serious sweetness, "but nobody could ever count my love for you. Shall I put the chops on, Jim?"

Out of his trance Jim seemed quickly to wake. He enfolded his Della. For ten seconds let us regard with discreet scrutiny some inconsequential object in the other direction. Eight dollars a week or a million a year—what is the difference? A mathematician or a wit would give you the wrong answer. The magi brought valuable gifts, but that was not among them. This dark assertion will be illuminated later on.

Jim drew a package from his overcoat pocket and threw it

upon the table.

"Don't make any mistake, Dell," he said, "about me. I don't think there's anything in the way of a haircut or a shave or a shampoo that could make me like my girl any less. But if you'll unwrap that package you may see why you had me going a while at first."

White fingers and nimble tore at the string and paper. And then an ecstatic scream of joy; and then, alas! a quick feminine change to hysterical tears and wails, necessitating the immediate employment of all the comforting powers of the lord of the flat.

For there lay The Combs—the set of combs, side and back, that Della had worshipped for long in a Broadway window. Beautiful combs, pure tortoise shell, with jewelled rims—just the shade to wear in the beautiful vanished hair. They were expensive combs, she knew, and her heart had simply craved and yearned over them without the least hope of possession. And now, they were hers, but the tresses that should have adorned the coveted adornments were gone.

But she hugged them to her bosom, and at length she was able to look up with dim eyes and a smile and say: "My hair grows so fast, Jim!"

And then Della leaped up like a little singed cat and cried, "Oh, oh!"

Jim had not yet seen his beautiful present. She held it out to him eagerly upon her open palm. The dull precious metal seemed to flash with a reflection of her bright and ardent spirit.

"Isn't it a dandy, Jim? I hunted all over town to find it. You'll have to look at the time a hundred times a day now. Give me your watch. I want to see how it looks on it."

Instead of obeying, Jim tumbled down on the couch and put his hands under the back of his head and smiled.

"Dell," said he, "let's put our Christmas presents away and

keep 'em a while. They're too nice to use just at present. I sold the watch to get the money to buy your combs. And now suppose you put the chops on."

The magi, as you know, were wise men—wonderfully wise men—who brought gifts to the Babe in the manger. They invented the art of giving Christmas presents. Being wise, their gifts were no doubt wise ones, possibly bearing the privilege of exchange in case of duplication. And here I have lamely related to you the uneventful chronicle of two foolish children in a flat who most unwisely sacrificed for each other the greatest treasures of their house. But in a last word to the wise of these days let it be said that of all who give gifts these two were the wisest. Of all who give and receive gifts, such as they are wisest. Everywhere they are wisest. They are the magi.

O. Henry, "The Gift of the Magi," *The New York Sunday World,* [originally titled "Gifts of the Magi], December 10, 1905, in Elegant Ebooks, http://www.ibiblio. org/ebooks/. HTML version by José Menéndez.

Contributing Authors

DIANA C. DERRINGER

Diana C. Derringer is a writer and blogger. Her work appears in more than thirty-five publications for children, youth, families, and seniors. These include *Clubhouse, Pockets, devozine, ENCOUNTER, Open Windows, The Upper Room, Country Extra, ParentLife, Missions Mosaic, The Christian Communicator,* and *Mature Living.* She also writes radio drama for Christ to the World Ministries. Devotions, drama, practical living, and lessons from life, poetry, and more find a home in her portfolio. Her drama collection, *Beyond Bethlehem and Calvary,* will be released in late 2015. She belongs to the American Christian Writers and the Kentucky State Poetry Society. Visit her at www.dianaderringer.com.

DIANNE GARVIS

Dianne Garvis is a recording artist, vocalist, author, and powerful motivational speaker. Her popular seminar, "Keys to Achieving Excellence," is the culmination of over twenty-five years of business experience in resort management and women's seminars. She's also the founder of The Good Neighbor Program, Inc., a community outreach program for neighbors in need.

Dianne is a graduate of Faith Christian University with a BA in Bible and Theology. She married the love of her life in 1994, and they are blessed with two miracle children.

KAYLEEN REUSSER

Kayleen Reusser has written twelve non-fiction children's books, magazine and newspaper articles, and several *Chicken Soup* stories. As a middle school librarian, she enjoys seeing a student's face light up with the appreciation of a good book. She has self-published a book of World War II stories and is a co-founder of two Christian writing groups. Kayleen speaks regularly to children and adults throughout the US on the importance of reading and writing. Learn more at www.KayleenR.com.

ALICE SULLIVAN

Alice Sullivan has worked in the book publishing industry since 2001 as a ghostwriter, author, writing coach, speaker, and editor. She has worked on over one thousand books, including eleven *New York Times* bestsellers. Some of her more notable clients include Dave Ramsey, Michael Hyatt, Bill Cosby, Thomas Steinbeck, Lee Greenwood, George Foreman III, Pam Tillis, and Judge Andrew Napolitano. She works with publishers, agents, and authors to develop books that are both entertaining and memorable. Visit her at www.alicesullivan.com.

Ten Questions for Planning Your Best Christmas Programs

1. Who is the audience?

2. How can you approach this Christmas in a fresh way?

3. Will you need special features including video, dance, music, and staging?

4. Will you want the audience to participate?

5. How long is the service?

6. Will you do one service for kids, youth, and adults?

7. Have times been set for services?

8. Will you need extra seating during the service?

9. What is your budget?

10. Do you need extra volunteers?

Church Survey

Thank you for using this Christmas program book. We would like to know what you think of the dramas. Please send us an email with your comments and your thoughts on how we might serve you better.

Paul Shepherd, Shepherd Publishing Services
paul@shepherdps.com

1. What did you think of the program book?

    Excellent   Average   Below Average

2. Which of the following would you like to see more of in future books?

    Dramas   Poems   Stories   Songs

3. Please tell us why you bought the book:

4. What other improvements would you like to see?

5. Would you use an Easter program book?

6. Would you use a year-round program book?

7. Which program book did you use?

    Kids   Youth   Adults

8. If you know of an author who would be interested in contributing to our books, please provide us their name and contact information:

9. Please share the name of your church, primary contact name, phone number, and email address: